Isaac Newton: The World in Motion

CHARACTERS

Mrs. Peters

Matt

Claire

Tammy Time

Greg

Tommy Time

Sir Isaac Newton

SETTING

In Mrs. Peters' classroom, present time; Cambridge University, England, 1687

READER'S THEATER

Mrs. Peters: All right, class, let's continue studying about Sir Isaac Newton and his three laws of motion. Isaac Newton was a British professor and the most famous scientist of his age. What he discovered about how the universe works was the basis for almost everything people knew for hundreds of years. Now, who remembers the experiment we did yesterday?

Matt: It was something with a card, penny, and glass, and that's all I remember.

Mrs. Peters: Well, that's a good start, Matt. But what happened with the card and the penny?

Claire: First you put a card on top of an empty glass, and then you put a penny on top of the card. When you pulled out the card, the penny fell straight down into the glass. Kerplunk! The penny didn't move away when the card moved.

Mrs. Peters: Very good, Claire. But why? That's always the important question.

Claire: I have no idea.

Mrs. Peters: Does anyone know?

Tammy: It states in the textbook that it has something to do with inertia. But I don't understand what inertia is.

Greg: I do, Mrs. Peters. My older sister is studying inertia in her high school science class. I think it's cool that we're studying the same thing.

Mrs. Peters: I'm glad you feel that way, Greg. So, tell us what inertia is.

Greg: Inertia is what Newton's first law of motion is about. It says that an object that is not moving will most likely stay that way. But an object that is already moving will keep moving unless someone or something stops it.

READER'S THEATER

Mrs. Peters: Very good. Or as the scientists say, "A body at rest tends to remain at rest, and a body in motion tends to remain in motion."

Matt: What do bodies have to do with the card and the penny?

Greg: A body is an object. Do you remember how Mrs. Peters pulled the card out?

Matt: Yeah. She pulled it out really fast, the same way magicians pull out a tablecloth without knocking over the glasses.

Greg: Right. The glasses stay on the table. They don't move away with the tablecloth. The penny didn't move either.

Claire: Are you saying that the penny was resting? Is that what you mean by an object staying at rest?

Greg: Pretty much. So, when Mrs. Peters pulled the card out, it just fell into the glass. The falling part was because of gravity.

Matt: What's the part about remaining in motion?

Greg: It's like when you're riding your bike, and you slam on the brakes. You're in motion, and your body tries to keep going forward. You have to grab on to your handlebars to keep from flying off the bike.

Mrs. Peters: Very good example, Greg. Now let's move on to Newton's second law of motion.

Matt: I don't want to move on. I have inertia.

Mrs. Peters: Very funny, Matt.

Tammy: I'm on Matt's side on this one. I'm having trouble connecting this stuff to the real world.

Tommy: Sounds like it's time for another *When Machine* trip, Mrs. Peters! Your lessons really come alive when we travel back in time and meet the people who came up with the ideas we're studying.

Tammy: A *When Machine* trip is exactly what we need! You should come along, Mrs. Peters.

Mrs. Peters: Me? But I never travel. I don't even take vacations from school. I'm much too scared to go back in time in your *When Machine*.

READER'S THEATER

Tommy: You're always telling us we should overcome our fears. Think how cool it would be to meet Sir Isaac Newton! You told us he was one of the most original thinkers in history. What better way to learn about his laws of motion?

Mrs. Peters: All right. I'll come, but so will Greg, Matt, and Claire. Let's see if science becomes more exciting when you get to meet a famous scientist.

Matt: I just lost my inertia, Mrs. Peters. Let's go!

Mrs. Peters: Okay, Tommy, set the *When Machine* for Cambridge, England, in 1687. That's when Isaac Newton announced and published his greatest scientific ideas.

Tammy: Fasten your seat belt, Mrs. Peters! You can close your eyes if you're frightened, but a *When Machine* trip only takes a few seconds.

Tommy: Okay, gang, we're off!

Tammy: And now, a few seconds later, here we are in England in 1687.

Mrs. Peters: And that's Isaac Newton sitting under an apple tree! Watch out for that falling—

Newton: Ouch! Every time I sit under this tree, an apple falls on my head. Oh, hello there, young people. Do I know you?

Mrs. Peters: We're taking a field trip from our school. We thought we would visit you to learn something about physics.

READER'S THEATER

Matt: Physics? Say, Greg, what's physics?

Greg: That's what they call the kind of science we've been studying. Physics is about the physical laws of the universe. Professor Newton, we've been learning about how you're developing new ideas in math and science. We're especially interested in your ideas about motion.

Newton: I'm so happy that my work interests you young people. I've devoted my whole life to these ideas. Actually, thinking about apples—how they keep hitting me on the head every time I sit under this tree—got me started. The reason is gravity, the same thing that keeps the moon traveling around Earth and Earth orbiting the sun. In fact, gravity is what keeps the whole universe from flying apart. From one apple to the entire universe, it's all gravity. Isn't physics fascinating?

Mrs. Peters: My students aren't so sure, Professor Newton. They think it's boring.

Newton: Boring? Ridiculous! It's physics that explains how the world works. How could that be boring? Take my first law of motion, for example.

Matt: A penny at rest tends to remain at rest, and a penny in motion tends to remain in motion.

Newton: That's close, young man. So you understand inertia. Now who wants to hear about my second law of motion?

Greg: I do, Professor Newton!

Claire: We all do, especially now that we're getting to see you in person.

Newton: Thank you, young lady. My second law states that force, mass, and acceleration are all related. What could be simpler than that?

Tommy: It doesn't sound so simple to me. I don't understand what force and mass and acceleration are.

Newton: Then let's break them down into separate components, or parts. What is force? Can anyone give me an example? Do you ever have to use force to do something?

Claire: Could force be how hard you push something?

Newton: Exactly! Then what do you think mass is?

READER'S THEATER

Matt: I think mass is how big something is! I've got more mass than Claire, because I'm bigger, right?

Newton: Almost, but don't confuse mass with weight. Weight is mass pulled by gravity. If you could climb the highest mountain, you'd keep your mass. Your size and shape wouldn't change, but your weight would be a bit less.

Matt: Why?

Newton: From that high up, the pull of gravity is less. When you have less gravity, you have less weight.

Claire: Like when astronauts in a spaceship float around in space.

Tammy: Be careful, Claire. One of the rules of traveling on the *When Machine* is that we can't talk about things from the future.

Greg: We understand mass, Professor. And acceleration is how fast you can make something go, right?

Newton: Not exactly. Acceleration is how fast you can increase the speed of something. For example, let's say I pull this wagon along at one speed: ten miles per hour. There is no acceleration because the speed remains constant—it is the same. To make the wagon go faster, I'd have to pull harder and use more force. Now let's say the wagon is moving at fifteen miles per hour.

Greg: It has accelerated by five miles an hour!

Newton: Correct. And I am out of breath! Now, if I add more mass to the wagon by filling it with rocks, it will get harder and harder to pull. But if I only use the same amount of force to pull, the wagon will decelerate—slow down. Put enough rocks in and I won't be able to move the wagon at all.

READER'S THEATER

Tammy: I see. If you change the amount of force on an object, it will change how fast it moves and the direction it goes. And if you change the mass or acceleration of that object, it will change the amount of force it takes to move it.

Newton: Correct. Force, mass, and acceleration are all related.

Tammy: But I still don't get the part about the apple and gravity.

Newton: Ah, let me explain. When you throw an apple into the air, what happens?

Isaac Newton: The World in Motion

Claire: It goes up, and then it falls down.

Newton: Exactly. What kind of force makes it go up?

Tommy: If you're the one who's throwing it, then you make the force.

Newton: Yes. Now what makes it come down? Where does that force come from?

Tammy: Gravity pulls it back down. Now I get it!

Mrs. Peters: Professor Newton, could you please tell us about your third law of motion? We need to get back to school.

Newton: For every action, there is an equal and opposite reaction. Every force creates an equal force in the opposite direction.

Tommy: I don't get that, Professor Newton. Could you use your wagon to explain it?

Newton: Imagine that you're inside the wagon and the wagon is standing still on a smooth, flat surface. You jump off the back as hard as you can. What happens to the wagon? Does it stand still? Does it move?

READER'S THEATER

Tommy: It rolls away.

Newton: In what direction?

Tommy: It rolls in the opposite direction that I jumped. Now I get it. I supplied force to the wagon when I jumped. It rolled in the opposite direction. That's the opposite part. But how could it be equal? The wagon's a lot bigger than I am.

Newton: Yes. But since the wagon has more mass than you do, it wouldn't move as far or as fast as you would. But the force would be the same.

Greg: Right. That's from the second law of motion.

Matt: Now I get it, too! This physics stuff is truly amazing, because it explains how and why things happen in our everyday lives. Everybody should know how important your laws of motion are, Professor Newton.

Newton: I agree! I'm going to sit under that tree and start writing the final version of my laws of motion. I'll wear a helmet, though, in case one of those apples falls on me again.

Tammy: Good-bye, Professor Newton. Thanks for taking the time to talk to us.

Newton: Thank you! I've enjoyed your enthusiasm and curiosity. Curiosity about how the world works is what keeps me going.

Mrs. Peters: Thanks for taking me on this trip, kids. Meeting Sir Isaac Newton was wonderful. But the best part was watching all of you discover how fascinating science can be.

READER'S THEATER

Tommy: The best part was having you come along with us, Mrs. Peters. You'll have to promise you'll come on another *When Machine* trip.

Mrs. Peters: You know, I think I will. There are so many amazing people in history I'd like to meet. I don't know why it took me so long.

Tommy: No more inertia for you, Mrs. Peters!

The End